How Sound Travel?

written by C. C. Paris

Contents

Harcourt

Orlando   Boston   Dallas   Chicago   San Diego

www.harcourtschool.com

In his room, Tommy blows his trumpet. Next door, Mrs. Smith covers her ears with her hands. Why?

2

The sound vibrations travel through the air and go right into Mrs. Smith's ears.

Tommy blows his trumpet even harder. The pitch is high, and the sound is loud.

Mrs. Smith bangs on her wall because she wants Tommy to stop playing. Does Tommy hear her?

No! The sound from Tommy's trumpet is too loud, but Tommy's cat near the wall hears. The cat hears the vibrations that travel through the wall. The cat runs and hides.

The cat brushes the glass of the fish bowl as it runs. Does the fish hear the brushing noise?

Yes! It hears the sound vibrations that travel through the water.
The fish swims and hides.

Tommy hears only the music his trumpet makes. It sounds wonderful to him.

Everyone else runs and hides!

Glossary

pitch   how high or low a sound is

sound   The kind of energy that lets you hear sound is made when things vibrate.

vibration   movement back and forth very fast

Index